THE ILLUSTRATOR'S LIBRARY
Printmaking

THE ILLUSTRATOR'S LIBRARY

Printmaking

BY DON BOLOGNESE AND ELAINE RAPHAEL

Franklin Watts
New York Toronto Sydney London
1987

The authors would like to express their gratitude
to Frank Sloan, for his guidance and for his
enthusiastic commitment to their work.

Library of Congress Cataloging-in-Publication Data

Bolognese, Don.
Printmaking.

(The Illustrator's library)
Includes index.
Summary: Introduces techniques for making
stencils, monoprints, woodcuts, and linoleum-block
prints.
1. Prints—Technique—Juvenile literature.
[1. Prints—Technique]   I. Raphael, Elaine.
II. Title.   III. Series: Don Bolognese. Illustrator's
library.
NE860.B58 1987   761   87-10417
ISBN 0-531-10316-1

C O N T E N T S

Introduction

This book is one of a series called the Illustrator's Library because each volume explores an artistic medium used by illustrators. Pencil, pen and ink, charcoal, and watercolor have been used for centuries to do artwork other than illustration. Printmaking, however, was developed especially for the purpose of illustration.

In Europe, around the middle of the 15th century (1450), a man named Johann Gutenberg invented and developed a method of printing from movable letters. At the same time the art of making paper was flourishing. These two developments made possible the first printed books. Until that time books had been made one at a time, with all of the text and illustrations written and painted by hand. Such books are known as illuminated manuscripts.

But the invention of printing changed all that. When that happened, hundreds and even thousands of copies of the same book could be produced. Suddenly everyone was writing and publishing books. And almost all of these books needed illustrations and decorations. Woodblocks, which were already being used to print decorative patterns on fabric, were immediately seen as the best way to provide printed illustration. Soon famous artists began designing the woodcuts. And as the art of the illustrated book developed, other forms of printmaking, such as etching, engraving, and lithography, were used to create illustrations.

Today printmaking is used by artists in many ways other than illustrating books. But as we explore these printmaking techniques, it is exciting to know that we are following in the footsteps of those artists who 500 years ago were the founders of modern illustration.

linoleum cut; black oil-base ink on rice paper

CHAPTER 1

Materials and Studio Setup

What is printmaking? Very simply it is the taking of an impression, or print, from an inked or painted surface.

For example, a print from a block of wood or linoleum is called a block print or a relief print. Many such prints can be taken from the same block. Hundreds of years ago the block print was the only way illustrations could be printed in books. Today, although most books are printed differently, the block print remains one of the favorite illustration techniques.

The monoprint is another popular printmaking technique. Unlike block printing, a monoprint produces only one print from the original design. Although the technique requires only simple tools and materials, it provides many opportunities for creative experimentation.

There are other forms of printmaking, such as etching, engraving, lithography, and silk-screening. However, because they require special equipment and materials, they should be studied in a studio or classroom setting.

linoleum cut; black and gray oil-base inks on rice paper

Monoprints and Stencil

The importance of monoprinting is its spontaneous and unpredictable nature. Great artists like Edgar Degas used it to explore different compositions and effects.

Today illustrators get exciting results from imaginative combinations of ink, paint, and unusual tools. Keep that in mind when you collect your materials. The list below is a starting point; it also contains many items needed for block printing:

Oil paints and oil-base block-printing inks
Brushes (bristle and stipple)
Old toothbrush
Printer's ink rollers (various widths)

Spatulas
Palettes, glass or plastic
Copper or zinc plates
Paint thinners (mineral spirits, turpentine, kerosene)
Stencil paper, tracing paper
Scissors and razor blades
Exacto knife (No. 11 blade)
Various papers, smooth and lightly textured
Cardboard
Baren for hand printing (A baren is a pad of twisted cord
    covered with paper or bamboo leaves, used to apply pres-
    sure to a woodcut)
One-coat rubber cement

Linoleum

The crisp line quality of a good linoleum cut can be achieved only with the use of sharp tools. Dull or poorly made tools are difficult to control. Students are usually encouraged to buy inexpensive tools to begin with. However, better-made tools really make it easier to learn proper cutting techniques. We suggest that you look at and try several types of tools before you purchase a complete set. Don't always buy the cheapest ones. A slightly more expensive set at the outset may save lots of money in the long run.

Most of the supplies for monoprinting can be used for linoleum and woodcutting. In addition you will need

 Linoleum tools
 Sharpening stone and light machine oil
 Water-base block-printing ink (as well as the oil-base inks)
 Linoleum, pre-cut, mounted on wood in various sizes;

or sheet linoleum, called "battleship linoleum" (sometimes available in stores that sell floor coverings).

Rice paper, block-printing proofing paper

Clear acetate, the type that can be painted on with tempera paint

Woodcut

Many of the supplies for linoleum cutting and printing can be used for woodcutting. Of course you will need wood. White or soft pine is a good choice. Try to get pieces that are knot-free, smooth, and not warped. As you gain more experience, you will want to try other kinds of wood. Some illustrators have used ordinary plywood very effectively. An important point to remember: oil-base inks work better on wood. Water-base ink tends to raise the grain on wood; the ink also dries out too quickly.

Some of the linoleum tools can be used on wood. You also will need wood filler (plastic wood).

CUTTING AREA

Setting Up a Studio

The ideal block-printing studio has two separate areas: one for cutting and one for printing. This separation helps to keep wood and linoleum chips from messing up the inking and printing process. If there is not enough space for two areas, the work space must be well cleaned before switching from one activity to another.

Make sure you have enough light. You may even want a small "task light" in your cutting area.

Safety and Health

Common sense and attention to the instructions on labels are all you need to avoid problems of health or safety. When working with any oil-base paints, inks, or solvents (thinner, turpentine), you should open windows or turn on an exhaust fan. *Never*

PRINTING AREA

work with these materials in a completely closed room (not even when the temperature outside is below zero). *Never* store solvents near any heat source. *Never* store inky or oily rags and paper towels overnight—get rid of them as soon as possible.

Cutting and Safety

When using a razor blade, a stencil knife, a woodcut tool, or any cutting instrument, keep your hand out of the cutting path. That sounds simple enough but sometimes it is too easy to forget or to become distracted. Or sometimes, because you are in a rush to finish something, it is hard to follow a basic safety rule. So always brace your block (linoleum or wood) against a support (see page 14) and keep your free hand behind the cutting edge of your tool.

C H A P T E R 2

Monoprint and Stencil

Monoprint is a direct and simple form of printmaking. A monoprint produces only one copy of the original work. Its value to the illustrator is in its painterly quality and its many accidental effects.

Discovering exciting accidents in one's own art is how an artist develops and grows. By examining an accidentally made effect, by understanding how it happened and learning how to repeat it, an illustrator develops new and unusual techniques.

Stenciling can be used as a technique by itself or combined with monoprint. In either case, stenciling lends itself to spontaneous solutions and unexpected effects. A stencil can produce more than one copy of itself, and it can be moved around on a page to produce multiple images.

So plunge right in, squeeze out some ink, and enjoy the expressiveness of these techniques.

monoprint; black oil-base ink on metal plate printed on 100% rag heavyweight paper

Found Objects

An exciting and simple way to get started is to print found objects. Use anything that can be inked and printed from. You'll like some results better than others, but this is how you become aware of the variety of textures that exist all around you.

The print on the opposite page was done in the following way: Each object was inked separately with a roller, then arranged on a clean metal or cardboard plate. Before printing the objects the artist used an old toothbrush to spatter some diluted ink on the plate. After printing the objects, the artist stenciled the black circles onto the print with a stipple brush and a plastic circle template.

monoprints: ordinary cookie cutter and kitchen spatula inked with black oil-base ink and printed on bond paper

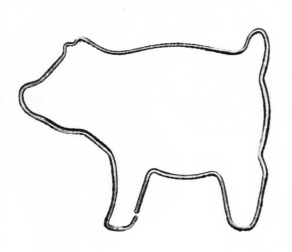

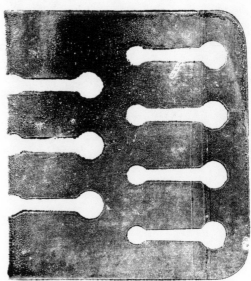

left: monoprint; black oil-base ink on metal plate printed on 100% rag heavy-weight paper

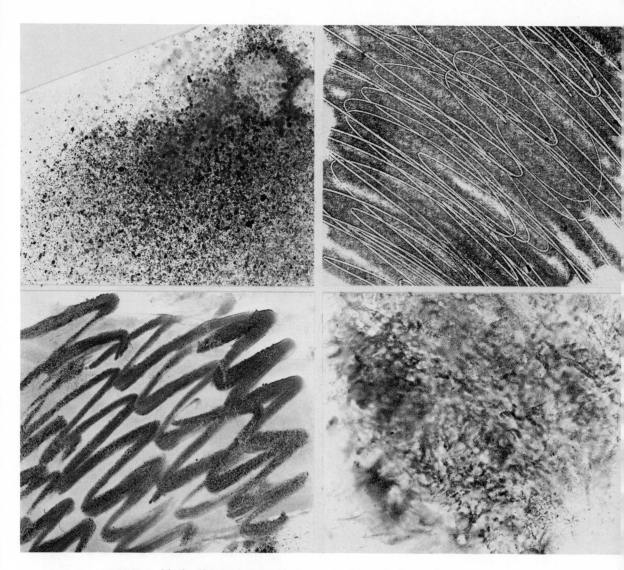

monoprints: black oil paint on metal plate printed on 2 ply strathmore paper

The Painted Monoprint

This form of monoprint is just like oil painting: any effect you create directly on the plate can be transferred to the paper. There are two points to remember. 1. Do not allow the oil paint or oil-base printing ink layer to become thick and uneven. Otherwise it will spread out when pressure is applied to the paper. 2. Do not allow the oil paint or oil-base printing ink to dry out. A few drops of kerosene in the paint mixture will help to keep it loose and wet.

The Drawn Monoprint

Now you are going to create a drawing with lines and details.

First, on a clean glass or metal plate, roll out a thin layer of black oil-base printing ink. Let it set for 20 to 30 minutes. In the meantime take one of your favorite drawings and make a pencil tracing of it. Then tape a sheet of ordinary drawing paper onto the inked plate. Next, tape the tracing to that paper. With a sharp H or HB pencil retrace the lines of your drawing. Try not to lean on the surface of the paper. When you are finished, lift the drawing paper.

left: pencil on tracing paper
right: monoprint; oil-base ink on ordinary drawing paper

Basically, the ink will transfer any mark you draw on the back of the paper. Use medium- or lightweight papers; smooth or textured, white or tinted, even papers that you have painted on. Experimenting will show you how dry or wet the ink should be to create the line quality you want.

Up to now you've been tracing your drawings. You can also draw freely onto the back of the drawing paper. You may achieve some exciting and spontaneous results. You may even discover some unusual effects. Illustrators experiment for just that reason: to increase their knowledge of techniques.

both monoprints: black oil-base ink on ordinary drawing paper

both monoprints: black oil-base ink on ordinary drawing paper

These illustrations developed out of the technique you've just been using. However, the artist has added a new touch, one that is both easy and effective.

She wanted the show people to appear in a dramatic but simple setting. She discovered she could create a black border by

rolling the ink directly onto the finished monoprint. She pro-
tected the area of the figures by covering the figures with clean
paper.

The result is a picture that suggests the spotlight atmosphere
of a circus.

Stencils and Cutouts

Stenciling is a great technique for producing graphic shapes and patterns. It is flexible and can easily be combined with other techniques. For example, in the illustrations of the two performers on pages 24–25, the artist used a rectangular cutout to create the black borders around the two figures.

A stencil has two forms. The first is the space that has been cut out of the stencil paper. This is like the ready-made stencils that are available at art stores. The second form is the cutout of the stencil.

The picture at the top of page 27 is an example of how a stencil can be used to create an image on a white page. In the picture at the bottom of page 27 the stencil cutout is used to color the background, leaving the silhouette of the figure on white paper. It is a very simple technique and a very effective one.

Pencil sketch; the first step in making a stencil. Note how simple the outlines are. The details such as facial features can be added to the stencil print afterwards with pen and ink.

stencil prints: oil base inks on 100% rag paper

Making Your Own Stencils

The first step in making stencils is the design. Since stencils have to be cut out of paper, you should keep the shape simple.

Next, transfer the design to the stencil paper. Try to use translucent stencil paper; it is easier for tracing onto and for cutting. If you use heavier, opaque stencil paper, transfer your design with carbon paper.

Cut out the design with an Exacto knife (blade No. 11 is good). Keep your free hand out of the path of your knife. Apply a firm,

A

B

even pressure on the knife and try to remove what you have cut out in one piece. Save the cutouts.

Tape the stencil to a sheet of paper. Holding the stencil against the paper with your fingers, use a stipple brush to apply the tempera paint or printing ink to the paper. Keep the paint or ink fairly dry; otherwise the wet pigment will seep under the edges of the stencil. The pigment can also be applied with a sponge, tissue, paper towel, rag, even a fingertip. Each of these materials will create a different texture.

A: pencil tracing of designs
B: actual stencil
   (translucent stencil paper)
C: stencil print;
   tempera paint on drawing paper

Designing with Movable Cutouts

Remember those cutouts you were supposed to save when you cut the stencils? Now you can use them.

Below are cutouts of various shapes—people, animals, and decorative borders. They have all been saved at different times. The illustrator can now spread them out and rearrange them to create a different design each time.

The designs can be printed in several ways: The cutouts can be stippled (see page 29). They can be pasted down (use *one-coat* rubber cement) and painted over with a large brush (use a dry-brush technique and make sure the paint isn't watery). You can also use a toothbrush—or even a can of spray paint—to spatter paint around the cutouts.

The important point is that cutouts and stencils give an artist many opportunities to test different design ideas.

There are many solutions to an illustration. The fun is in discovering those solutions.

right: stencil-print; black oil-base ink on 100% rag heavyweight paper

CHAPTER 3

The Woodcut

A good storyteller is always looking for new ways to add interest to a story; a good illustrator does the same, constantly exploring techniques and methods for creating unusual effects.

The woodcut is one such technique. It offers sharp contrasts, expressive linear quality, and rich textures. These characteristics lend themselves to the illustration of many types of stories and especially to those with a high level of drama. The woodcut also favors bold, simple, and graphic designs, designs that would be effective as book covers and posters.

The other aspect of the woodcut is its texture. Many illustrators use woodcuts especially for their decorative grains. They sometimes base an entire design on the wood texture. Some artists approach woodcuts very directly and will cut them without any preliminary sketches. "Bridge fireworks" was done exactly that way, spontaneously.

Your approach will depend on the kind of story you want to tell.

woodcut; black oil-base ink on rice paper

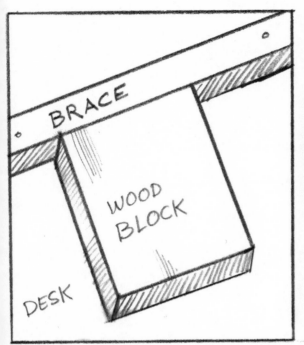 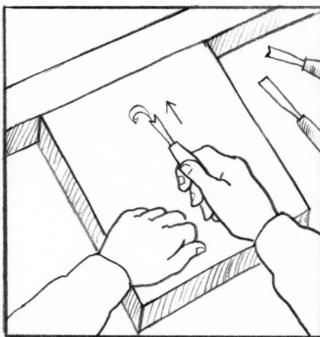

The Studio Setup—Safety First

If possible, set aside a desk (or desk area) just for cutting. Attach a stick or board to the surface to act as a brace for your woodblock (see illustration). *Do not* attempt to cut your block without the brace because the pressure of the cutting tool will move the block unless it is secured in this manner. When using a gouge or chisel, *keep your free hand and arm behind the cutting edge of the tool. Never cut toward your free hand.* (See above.) Instead, turn the block so that the cutting edge is pointed away from your free hand.

Cutting with a knife sometimes requires that you draw the knife toward you (see illustration). In that case remember these two points: 1. Never place your free hand in the path of the knife. 2. *Do not* use too much force or pressure. The cut does not have to be very deep.

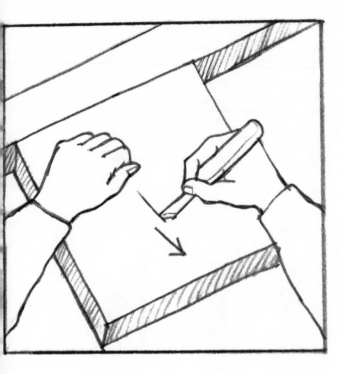

Note that the wood block is always firmly against the brace and the free hand should always be out of the tools' path.

Finally, keep your cutting area free of unnecessary objects (soda cans, glasses of milk, drawing pads, etc.). When using a book or picture for reference, place it on a separate surface near you (or tack the picture to a wall).

Tools

All artists' tools need caring for; brushes must be thoroughly washed, pen points cleaned, and pencils sharpened. Woodcutting tools are no exception. When you purchase your set of tools, remember to ask for a good sharpening stone. Some of them even have V- and U-shaped grooves. That and a can of light oil are all you need. Make it a practice to sharpen your tools regularly. A sharp tool not only creates better and cleaner lines, it is also a safer tool because it is easier to guide and control.

Kinds of Tools

V gouges: These come in various sizes. The smaller ones are used to create thin lines. They should not be pushed too deeply into the wood. As a general rule a cut should be deep enough only to get below the surface. V gouges cut best with the grain. Cutting across the grain usually tears the wood, creating a ragged line. However, it is an effect that you may want to use sometime.

U gouges: These tools also vary in width. They produce a soft, rounded edge at the beginning and end of the stroke. U gouges also will not cut cleanly across the grain.

CHISEL　　　　**U GOUGE**　**V GOUGE**　**KNIFE**

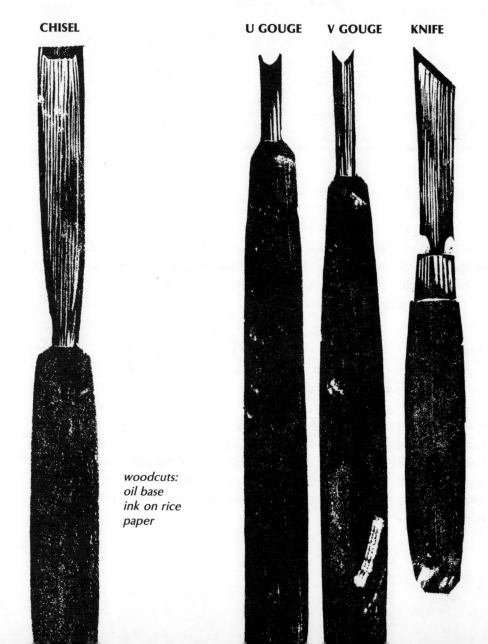

*woodcuts:
oil base
ink on rice
paper*

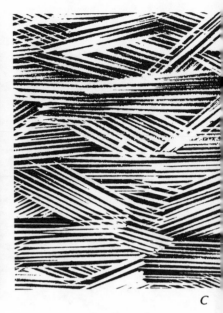

A

B

C

woodcut textures: oil-base ink on rice paper
A: small V gouge (light cut) with the grain
B: large V gouge (deep cut) with and against grain
C: small V gouge cut at slight angle to grain

Knives: Many woodcutters consider the knife their most important tool, especially when cutting across the grain. The technique is simple. To cut a thin white line you make two cuts. This will produce a cut that looks as if you used a V gouge. To make a black line or shape, angle the knife to avoid undercutting the surface (see illustration).

Chisel: Use a chisel to clear out wood from between shapes and lines. Sometimes it is easier to clear areas first with a wide, shallow U gouge. Then use a flat chisel to take off peaks that are left by the U gouge. The best way to prevent the accidental removal of lines and edges is to work cautiously. Do small areas and avoid deep gouging.

Other Tools and Textures

Wood can also be poked and punched with various objects to create textures. A nail is one such example. Use different sizes of nails to produce a variety of holes. Use found objects that can be hammered into the surface of the wood to create textures. Sanding the wood can sometimes bring out the grain texture.

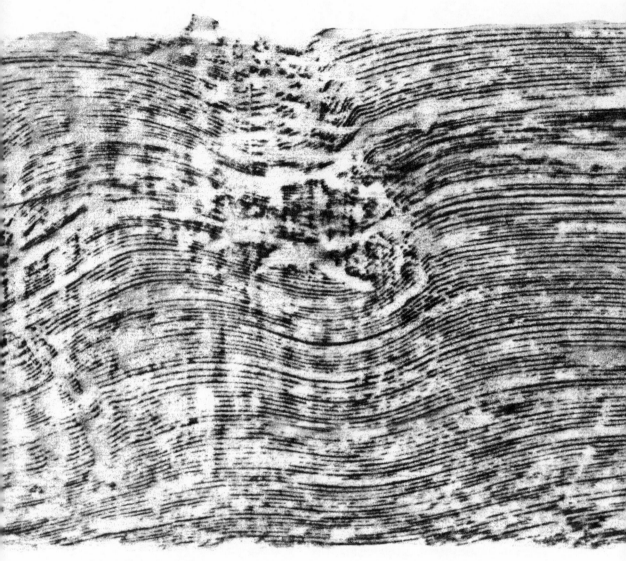

graphite stick rubbing on rice paper

Design and Transfer Techniques

A woodblock already has a design on its surface—the wood grain. Try this experiment: Put a piece of printing paper (rice paper) on the uncut wood block. Rub the back of the paper with a graphite stick. The texture you see is the wood grain. Some illustrators like to use this natural pattern as part of their design. Grain is different for each type of wood, and it also varies from one block to another.

Designing Directly on the Woodblock

Design your first woodcut by drawing directly on the wood. First ink the surface of the woodblock with an oil-base ink. Rub off the excess ink. This will give the wood an even, dark tone. When the block is dry, draw on it with any light-colored pencil or pastel pencil; even white tempera paint can be used. You will cut away the white lines and shapes you've drawn.

When you print your design, it will be the reverse of what you've drawn.

In your first designs keep the shapes simple. Experiment with your tools. Create a variety of patterns and textures with only short strokes (see fish scales).

woodcut; oil-base ink on rice paper

Note that a picture drawn directly on the block will print in the opposite direction—see print at bottom right.

INKED BLOCK ↑

PALETTE ↑

Printing

Pulling the first print from a woodblock is always a surprise. The print is never exactly what you thought it would be. This doesn't bother printmakers. Surprises are part of the experience and the fun of printmaking.

Part of the enjoyment comes from the fact that block printing is not complicated or difficult. There are, however, a few things you should do to get a good print. Begin by preparing the printing and inking areas. They must be free of dirt and wood chips that might get stuck in the ink or on the rollers. Remember to brush off chips from the woodblock.

The block printing paper should be cut to the right size and stacked. The less you handle the paper (especially with ink-stained fingers), the better. Squeeze some oil-base ink onto a palette. Mix it a bit with a metal spatula. Put a small amount on a clean area of the palette. Roll out the ink. It should cover the palette area evenly, with no globs.

Begin inking the woodcut. The first coating of ink will sink into the wood. Repeat the inking and rolling procedures until the block has an even coating. Place a sheet of paper on the inked block. With the palm of your hand press it evenly onto the block.

Use a baren or a smooth wood surface (wooden spoon, tool handle) to rub the paper firmly. The stickiness of the ink should keep the paper from moving and sliding as you rub. Use a circular motion and even pressure over the whole block. Now and then lift a corner of the paper to check on your progress. With experience you will know when you've rubbed enough.

PAPER

Be careful not to rub too hard; the paper might tear.

woodcut: oil-base ink on rice paper

Two Illustration Projects

It's great fun to do an illustration of a real "bad guy." Is there anyone meaner than Scrooge? Or more hardhearted? "Hard"—a good word to describe Scrooge. But how would you illustrate him?

First the artist had to make a basic decision. Should Scrooge look straight at us? Or should he turn his head and look at us out of the corner of his eye?

This is the value of sketches: They allow the artist to consider different solutions. In this case the artist first thought a front view would be best. After doing several sketches the artist changed his mind. Scrooge in profile seemed meaner and "harder" than Scrooge head-on.

The artist then did a full-size sketch on tracing paper with a black felt marker. After making a few corrections he transferred the design to the block.

Here are the directions: 1. Blacken the wood surface. 2. Tape the full-size final sketch to the block with *the drawing side against the wood*, so that it faces the opposite direction from which it was drawn. 3. Place a white carbon sheet between the wood surface and the drawing. 4. Trace the design onto the block. Check occasionally to see that all of the lines are being transferred.

thumbnail pencil sketches

felt marker on tracing paper with white tempera paint highlights and corrections

Cutting

The artist cut with the grain. Large V gouges created the pointed and threatening pattern (left top half of picture on page 44). Small V gouges were used on the collar of Scrooge's coat. And various U gouges were used elsewhere.

The darks and lights were designed to focus attention on Scrooge's face, especially his eye. The artist was so sure of his design that he cut almost the entire design before making a print. All he made were a few pencil rubbings as guidelines to

both woodcuts: oil-base ink on rice paper

cutting Scrooge's features. When he saw the first print, he was not pleased. Something bothered him about the design. Can you guess what it was?

Here's a clue. Cover the light areas of Scrooge's hat with black paper. Do you see any difference in Scrooge's face? The illustrator did. He decided that the light texture (right half) on Scrooge's hat competed with Scrooge's eye for attention.

Fortunately, with wood there is a way to

rubbing graphite stick on rice paper

correct such a mistake. First, clean the block well. Then fill the mistakes with wood filler (follow directions on the can). When that dries, sand the filler down to the level of the woodblock surface. Use fine sandpaper wrapped around a small flat block of wood. Sand only in the direction of the grain.

Print the block to see how well the holes are filled. You may have to add some more filler or sand the block before the repair job is complete. Don't worry about making mistakes; they can be corrected.

However, this mistake did teach Scrooge's illustrator a lesson. He decided to proceed more cautiously in his next print by pulling more proofs during the cutting stage.

Mystery and Intrigue

The scene is a forest. The hero of the story is about to meet a mysterious stranger. The meeting that is about to take place will involve the hero in a web of lies and intrigue.

The illustrator of this story did not want to do the obvious: a picture of the characters meeting. Instead, she wanted to create a setting of mystery and entanglement.

Her sketchbooks and her bookshelves contained many drawings and photos of trees. She looked at them all. She went for a walk in the woods. It was winter. A thin layer of snow covered the ground. The dark tree trunks looked like lonely cloaked figures. Above her, the leafless branches criss-crossed against a cloudy sky looked like a giant net. An idea began to take shape.

The drawing below is her first sketch:

The Clear-Acetate-Overlay Method of Design

Her next step was a full-size drawing. She decided on a sketch technique well suited to woodcut.

First, she inked and printed the woodblock she intended to use. She then taped a sheet of clear acetate to the print. She used a fine watercolor brush and white tempera paint to create the design on the acetate. Because the paint could be washed off *and* repainted easily, she was able to develop and change the design until she was satisfied. Another advantage came from seeing the design develop on top of the actual wood-grain texture.

left: felt marker on tracing paper

right: white tempera on acetate sheet taped over a rice paper print of uncut wood block

46

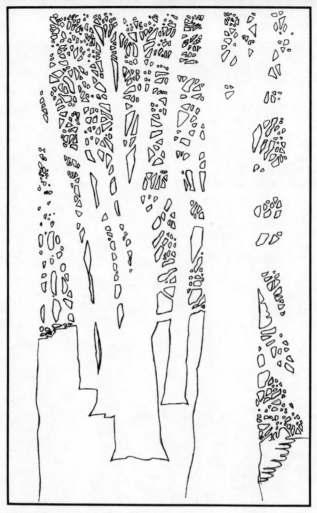

pencil tracing (reduced size)

When she was sure of her design, the artist did a pencil tracing of it. She then turned over the tracing and taped it in position on the woodblock. She placed a white carbon sheet under the tracing and with an HB pencil traced the lines so that they transferred to the woodblock.

The cutting itself was simple. For most of the small white shapes in the "web" of branches the artist used a small V gouge. Sometimes she used a knife to cut a straight or curved line across the grain. She used a large U gouge to clean out the white spaces between the trunks.

The interesting thing about this woodcut is that although it looks very complicated and difficult it was neither. It is, however, an effective and dramatic picture because the artist knew how to let the medium work for her. She made good use of the woodcut's texture and dark-and-light potential.

woodcut: oil-base ink on rice paper

C H A P T E R 4

Linoleum

Bold black shapes, sweeping curves, sharp, white accents, textures that jump off the page. These are only some of the artistic effects that are possible with linoleum.

Like the woodcut, the linoleum cut is a medium with great potential for dramatic storytelling. In fact, both types of block print are alike in many ways. But they are different, too. Those differences are a result of the materials themselves. Wood has a grain and a texture; linoleum has neither. Each block of wood is different; all linoleum blocks are alike. Wood warps and sometimes cracks; not linoleum. Wood can be repaired; this is not so easy with linoleum (it is sometimes necessary to replace and recut the entire area).

Those are some of the practical differences. From an artistic point of view the differences can be seen by comparing two illustrations: "Scrooge" on pages 44 and 45 and "Ethan Allen" (opposite page). Everything in Scrooge is more angular, even the curved lines. The wood grain is visible in the darkest areas, and the edges of lines have a splinter-like quality.

The illustration of Ethan Allen is full of flowing curves in both the white and black. The black areas are dense, and textures are created by the tool rather than by the grain.

Once you begin working on both wood and linoleum, you will discover how each suits your talent and objectives.

linoleum cut: 3 tones of oil-base ink printed on 100% rag heavyweight paper

The Studio Setup

Follow the same procedures as for woodcutting. Remember the *safety first steps:*

1. Set aside a special area or desk for cutting.
2. Attach a stick to it to brace your linoleum block while cutting.
3. Never put your free hand or arm in the path of your cutting tool.
4. Keep the cutting area free of unnecessary objects.
5. Keep your tools sharpened. Remember, a dull tool is more difficult to guide and control.

both pages: linoleum cut: oil-base ink on rice paper
Can you pick out where "U" and "V" gouges were used?

Tools and Textures

One of the pleasures of working in linoleum is experimenting to see how many textures are possible.

The place to begin is with each tool. Try cutting with very light pressure; this produces a shallow cut. Then increase the pressure slightly; the cut will be deeper and the stroke wider. Never gouge too deeply. That lessens your control and can cause you to cut through the burlap backing on the linoleum.

Use long strokes and short ones. Cross them; mix V gouges with U gouges. Notice how the beginning and end of each stroke is a defined shape. By varying the space between strokes you can create lighter or darker patterns.

linoleum cut; black line technique using a variety of gouges and a knife; oil-base ink on rice paper

Black or White Line

As you've already noticed, the simplest way to make a line on linoleum is with a small V gouge. When this is printed, it will produce a white line. White drawing lines are the opposite of what we are used to. Usually, artists' tools, such as pencils, pen and ink, brushes, charcoal, produce dark lines on a light background. People expect to see scenes illustrated that way: dark objects on light backgrounds.

The book illustrators of the Middle Ages who developed the block print knew the expectations of their readers. Their solution was the black-line technique, much more difficult than the white-line technique. It requires cutting enough of the block to leave a black line or shape.

Here two pictures of the same design clearly show the difference. You can try this experiment with a simple design. The black-line technique requires a more detailed drawing as well as more control in the cutting.

As you practice and become surer of your technique, you will discover how to mix both techniques in the same illustration. Today artists go from one to the other depending on what effect they want. Their only concern is to make an interesting picture.

left: linoleum cut; white line technique using small V gouge; oil-base ink on rice paper

Because the block print is so closely connected with the first printed books, people often associate block prints (linoleum and wood) with historical subjects. In fact, scenes from the past such as knights, castles and colonial life offer excellent opportunities for working in linoleum.

The picture you will see develop over the next few pages is one example. It is for the title page of a book on knights and chivalry.

Sketches

The picture began the way most illustrations do—as a sketch. The illustrator used a black marker as a sketch tool because the dark-and-light quality of a marker resembles the effect of a block print. Pen or brush and ink are also effective in preparing sketches for block prints.

felt marker on layout paper

pencil on tracing paper

White lines and details were painted on black areas by using a bleed-proof white tempera paint. The finished sketch was then traced onto tracing paper.

The illustrator then transferred the drawing to the block with black carbon paper. Remember that the tracing should be turned facedown on the block. The final print will then face the same direction as the original drawing.

Cutting

Where do you begin cutting? That is a good question that artists often ask themselves. There are many answers; here is what the illustrator of the "Knight" picture replied:

"I begin cutting areas I'm most sure of. In this picture, for example, I had a very clear idea of how I wanted the overall silhouette to appear. I started by cutting all of the main forms, using a small V gouge. In places like the face I used a knife to get into all of the corners. After completing the outline I used a wide U gouge to cut away the linoleum around the outline. During this process I took pencil rubbings to check on my progress. Eventually I also pulled an ink proof.

rubbing: Detail showing how artist checked his progress—note that rubbing and print face in opposite directions.

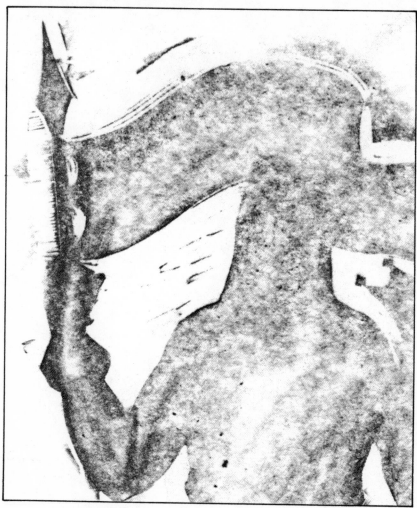

"The proof was now my guide. I have often made changes in the design after seeing the first proof. For example, I decided that the heraldic lion was more decorative than the crusader's symbol. I'll also test certain details by painting them in white on clear acetate taped on the proof" (see pages 46–47 and 60–61).

The point to remember is that once the block is cut and a proof has been pulled, that print becomes all-important. Although you may have worked very hard on certain details of a sketch, if the print itself seems to need a different solution, don't be afraid to change your design. And as this illustrator recommends, test new ideas by using a clear acetate overlay.

linoleum cut: Detail showing how figures are outlined. Oil-base ink on rice paper

above: detail of tempera painting on acetate
left: linoleum cut with acetate overlay

Printing

Printing linoleum blocks is very similar to printing woodblocks. One difference is that linoleum will not absorb as much ink as wood will. For that reason be careful not to roll too heavy a layer of ink on the linoleum block. The small details will fill in, and the print will appear "heavy."

The ink should be "tacky," not too oily. If your ink is oily and loose, put a glob of it onto ordinary brown paper (paper bag); the extra oil will be absorbed. Then transfer the ink to a palette and roll it out evenly. Use a hard-rubber roller that is big enough to cover a good part of the block in one pass. Example: on an 8-by-10-inch (20-by-25-cm) linoleum block you should use a 4-inch (10-cm) roller. This helps control the amount of ink that gets on the block.

When the block is sufficiently inked (after a few inkings you will know when there is enough ink), place a piece of rice paper on the block. Press it in place with your hand and then rub with a baren or smooth, rounded wooden object (see pages 40–41 for a full description).

The Final Stage

Between the first printing (previous page) and the final print (opposite page) the artist made many changes from the original design on page 57. If you compare them, you can see many details that are different. But the change of detail is not the important point. The overall effect is the illustrator's main concern.

What was the artist trying to convey?

The artist's biggest hope was to convey a sense of adventure and romance. He tried to capture the feeling of a time when knights battled dragons to rescue "damsels in distress" or when courtly and beautiful ladies chose knights as their champions.

The artist realized that his goal was better achieved by leaving out or changing many of the details he had planned to include. The helmet he finally put on the knight is more symbolic of knighthood than are the knight's facial features. But the artist's most important design decision was the emphasis on a strong contrast between the dark figures and the white background. The dramatic lighting is the key to the illustration's spirit of adventure and romance.

The pictures in this book are playful, moody, decorative, mysterious, dramatic, textural, and romantic. They are by artists whose imaginations have been inspired by the experimental and graphic qualities of printmaking, the art form developed primarily for illustration.

linoleum cut: oil-base ink on rice paper

Index